TWO DIFFERENT WORLDS

FRANCIS XAVIER

Copyright © 2023 Francis Xavier

First Edition

NEWMAN SPRINGS PUBLISHING
320 Broad Street
Red Bank, NJ 07701

First originally published by Newman Springs Publishing 2023

ISBN 979-8-88763-187-5 (Paperback)
ISBN 979-8-88763-188-2 (Digital)

Printed in the United States of America

Pulling into the parking lot, I look into my rearview mirror, and the face looking back at me says, "Well, Sally boy, let's see what today has in store for you." I was facing the multiple choice of glass doors to enter in.

I marvel at the number of people streaming in and out like a colony of ants. I'll take the middle with the revolving doors. Those doors always remind me of the slapstick humor of people going around and around. I was then walking down the seemingly endless corridor to the huge cherrywood double doors in front of me marked Pan Am Import and Export. The first step I take into the office, I sink into the two inches of rug that looks like a sea of Hershey's chocolate. The greeting is always the same no matter how many times I go there. "Good day. Nice to see you again. How can I help you?"

Mara looking like a marble sculpture of the prefect greets me in a cold manner.

"Sir James has been waiting for you, so go right in."

Behind his oversized oak desk sat Sir James—impeccable as ever. Nothing out of place with him or the office.

In keeping with his refined English upbringing, he says, "Do have a seat."

Then comes, "What the fuck took you so long to get here." With that opening line, all those images fade. I'm standing in front of Jimmy *Cold Cuts* inside of his Brooklyn delicatessen. The beautiful and cold Mara that greeted me is actually Carmine—5 foot 4 inches, 275 lbs., son of Jimmy Cold Cuts.

The long corridor in reality was rows of wire racks on either side filled with chips, bread rolls, and groceries.

"So, Jimmy, what do you have for me?"

"Sally boy, only the old man and Jimmy still call me that. How would you like to take a trip to London?"

"Jimmy, sometimes I get lost coming to your deli, and I was born two miles from here."

"Are you finished crying?"

"Do you want me to tell you about the trip?"

"Okay, tell me how much, and I might consider the trip."

Jimmy says it's nothing to consider; it's for the old man. "You get about eight grand. Everything else is covered."

"Okay, I need the money. What do you need?"

"The old man needs you to send a message to his associate in London. The guy you set the deal up for him to get the diamond and stones. What happened? Everything was going smooth."

"Everyone was making money."

"Well now he needs you to deliver a message."

"Why can't he call or send a letter? It's much cheaper."

"Don't be stupid. You know the message he wants to send. I will make all the arrangements for you. You just go and enjoy your mini vacation and see London.

"You go to the hotel first and check in, and I will give you a number to call when you get there. His brother will pick you up, and you go to their house. Bonner won't be there. Give his brother the message when you get there. There is nothing to negotiate. Just deliver the message. Take a cab back to the hotel, check out, go to the airport, and catch the next flight back to New York."

"Okay, but what went wrong with the deal?"

"He never sent the last shipment. The Nigerian said that the old man was way ahead with the profits.

"Sally boy, don't forget the draft board story. Your father did not want you playing in the jungle, and you were getting married in two years. You went to Fort Hamilton, passed your physical, were marked IA, and sent home to wait to be called. The old man pulled strings, and you were reclassified. You got to stay stateside. Personally, Sally boy, you were better off going to the jungle instead of getting married. I know, but it would not have mattered. She would have got me when I came home."

"So we are set. I will get this trip together for you. It was so easy, all nice and neat. I just looked over the emails I had. It was all self-explanatory."

This all started years before I was born.

Before the Great Depression, 1926, my father, Raymond Scalini, came to America again. He was actually born 1907 in Mott Street, New York, and his family went back when he was three years old.

I could never figure out how a family of painters in a small town in Italy could travel back and forth so easy.

He came from the same small town as his friend, Vito Genovese, so there was no problem for him to get work. His wife came over in 1930. He needed a better job, so Vito set him up as a foreman in Todd's shipyard in Brooklyn.

Vito set him up in apartments he owned. The family grew and so did the jobs he took on. Running alcohol, collections, numbers, etc. When my brothers were old enough, they worked with my father.

Early on, Vito had the idea to set the Scalini family up as a neutral clearing house for any overlapping business from the five families—sort of a mob Switzerland. This worked for a short period.

I met Vito once when he came over the house. I was young, and I hardly remember. My father spent more time with Vito's brother, Carmine. The stories I heard and the people I met growing up amazed me.

My brothers drifted away from any involvement, but I always went around with my father when I could. It was an amazing education.

I remember one meeting where we went to a restaurant in Queens called Vesuvio. We walked in and my father waved to some people standing around. They nodded to him, and we went to a table where some guy about my father's age was sitting. He stood up shook my father's hand and said thank you for coming, Don Raimondo.

It seems this guy owned appliance stores and was looking to expand. He needed a large amount of capital for what he wanted to do. I thought this was going to be a loan where the big boys were going to get some large weekly vig money (vig weekly interest). Instead, he was cleaning mob money. So instead of charging for the cleaning, he wanted it to be no charge for cleaning and no loan repayment.

Evidently my father knew what he wanted this meeting for. He had already got the approval from the powers above to make this deal. Both parties were happy except me. Their idea for closing a deal was some guy comes over with three espressos and Anisette with pastries. Nothing like the big corporation lunch deals. No drinks except big lunch champagne. I asked my father what does he get from this deal. Nothing. You do the right thing, they don't forget. Whenever something comes up, you ask for help. There are no questions asked as to how my father did it all—a little piece here and there. His method worked because in 1958, we moved from a Brooklyn apartment to a large house in Queens; fourteen thousand dollars in cash. It had trees, grass, and very little concrete. My father's method and painting business paid off. We lived pretty good.

I went with my father to my cousin Tony's used car lot, and the regular crew was there. Tony was involved with the garbage and restaurant unions. While we were there, Tony said he was ordering lunch, what did everybody want. I said, "Give me a sausage and pepper hero." Everybody laughed. I asked, "What's so funny about a sausage and pepper hero?" He said, "Hoffa went missing. So nobody orders sausage or meatball anything." They all laughed again, but the other six people did not order any meat heroes.

Maybe it was a joke, who knows.

Tony introduced me to a guy named Jackie and told me to work with him. Jackie said, "We will sit down next week." There were so many activities going on and money coming in it was unbelievable. Chop shop's flood-damaged cars were all reconditioned, rebuilt, given new VIN numbers, and sold for a thousand percent profit. They had connections everywhere. Tony reminded me to meet with Jackie and he told me another friend of ours named Lucky would be calling me.

Jackie was not a made guy, but an important link in the money chain that fed the organization.

Jackie's deal was a commission on window cleaning and installation bids in Brooklyn Bronx and mainly Manhattan. He wanted me to collect for him. He said he was getting too old to drive around. How much is in it? Four to six cents per window. "You're kidding. You can't buy lunch for that," I said. He said, "You know how many fucking windows there are? All these bids are rigged. Any install the big boys get is one to two dollars per window. If you bring anyone new in, you get a piece." I went to work and started making my own connections.

I started doing favors helping with some issues that the well-to-do did not want to dirty their hands with. That's how I made friends in Wall Street; with people like the feds, police, and even the CIA. I was feeling the power like the people I saw growing up.

Me and my friend Tommy opened up an after-hours club in the industrial area in Suffolk. We were making money, but I spread the word on the off nights that it was a strip club. Now we were making good money. A real strip club required a liquor license, permits, taxes, etc. Word spread, and people who wanted companionship and needed discretion came to me. Talk about making high-level connections.

I expanded to a Polish hall in the NASSAU county. Sold 250 tickets and brought in strippers and party girls. We took in 8 grand every party, and we held these parties every 3 months. By the third party, we were pulling down 15,000 dollars profit and were selling 400 tickets. I did this for a year and then gave it to the guys who helped me start it.

I wanted to work with Tony's friend, Lucky—he had some bigger ideas. He had connections in Colombia where he was from. He said when he gets it together, we will work together on it.

I know my father always stressed about respect and respect for those who went before you. You will always be respected. He was right, and I thought about the fact that all my father's civilian friends (non-mob) always referred to him as Don Raimondo. He was not a don as in the mob hierarchy, but his old-time mob people also referred to him as Don Raimondo. This was the way to be.

Things did not always go smooth for me. Back in the '70s, my good friend's brother owned a club on Long Island called The Castle. It was a replica inside and out, like a European castle. Nicky called me one day and asked what he should do. Seems a guy was coming around claiming big-time contacts. He said he bought the guy drinks when he came in, but now was saying the people above him wanted money each week to keep the place open. "Tell him you have to talk to your silent partner and tell me when he is coming," Nicky said.

I told Nicky, "Don't worry. He is nobody with no contacts—just a wannabe." So he comes in one night after closing. He is a big guy and dressed for the part. I asked how much was he going to pick up and for who. He says, "Who the fuck are you?"

"A friend looking out for a friend."

Nicky gets nervous easily, so he took him to a table. I go to the bar and pour a drink. I hear Nicky talking, and the big guy starts getting loud. I turn around in time to see him hit Nicky over the head with a slapjack (lead encased in leather). I run over to help Nicky, and I see him reach into his jacket. Pretty sure he was not reaching for a smoke. So before he got his hand out, I had my gun out and put two into him. He dropped like somebody pulled the rug from under him. Nicky starts screaming, "You just killed a made guy! What do we do now?"

"Relax, he ain't nobody." I looked around up front; the entrance had to be repaired. There was mortar, sand, lime, and new slate. We dug out the area, dumped him in, poured the lime, and mixed the mortar. Nicky wanted to go through his wallet to see who he was. I said, "No. If you know his name and someone asks for him, you will get freaky." So I poured the mortar mix and set the new slate. Nobody ever came around looking for him.

The kicker to this story is, they shot a movie called *Married to the Mob*. Opening scene, you see a mobster walking into the castle. You can't make this stuff up.

I wanted to be a made guy, but they said the books were closed. Just as well. I saw no one made out—only bosses or underbosses made any kind of living.

My cousin Greg Pistone was a made guy. He was not the same Pistone in the movie with Pacino Donny Brasco. He did a lot of work but ended up broke, lost his house, and had to scrounge around to support his family.

There is no loyalty; you have to plan ahead in this business.

One of the contacts I made was Rinaldo. He was the local go-to guy for cocaine and weed. He was a good guy, and he asked if I needed anything. I told him, "I don't do drugs, and I don't even smoke. You would be perfect in this business." Most dealers start off good but then start using their own product. They use up the profits then dip into the main stash, and now they are in the hole for money. When we sat down, he showed me how it all worked. He gave me a list of his customers, so I worked with him. The shocking part to me was who his customers were. Doctors, lawyers, Wall Street people… The one Wall Street guy I met was Franco who worked for J. A. Scott Brokerage. He gave me stock tips, and I gave him his coke free. I did not have the big money, but doing the small trades I was able to take my wife and kids on a cruise and on Disney trips.

I traded this stock information to my doctor, lawyer, and professional. I made even more high-end contacts. My brother-in-law, Teddy, had a huge number of contacts. His cousins were the Gallos. Anything you needed you asked Teddy—he always knew someone somewhere. We went to lunch at his friend's house, and he introduced me to this old guy in his nineties, Tony De Gregorio. Turns out his father in the 1920s and 1930s was big-time connected; he was Gaspare De Gregorio. Tony still had his hand in the mix. I also met this guy, Ralph. He is eighty, and we got to talking how he was having trouble collecting the money he had out in the street. I thought about my father when he said respect for the old timers who went before you. I told Ralph I would help him collect. He said he would take his wife to Villa Roma once a year, but things were tough. I lent him twenty thousand to put on the street, and he told the people he had a partner. We drove around and collected his old and new collections. He was happy, said it was like old times. He took his wife to Villa Roma. His family was glad I helped him out. Years later, he passed away, but I was glad I helped.

That one was for you, Pop! I was never invited to the service they held for Ralph. I guess people like me are good to know, but not to be invited to pay my respect. That's life!

Doing all this was not easy. I had to do all that while holding a full-time job, raising a family, and trying not to go to jail or get killed by some rival.

You know that saying, "I got a guy who knows a guy"? Well that worked well for me.

People always coming to me for help.

One of my professional connections asked if I could help a friend of his who was a big shot in a hospital in Suffolk. The hospital was going to do a major renovation, and he wanted his friend's company to get the bid. Why does he want to get involved for a friend with something that can put him away?

He needs money. He is overextended, and he is seeing another woman. How big can this job be that he thinks this will solve all his problems? I think he said rough estimate ninety-five million.

Okay, I will talk to him and let him know if anything goes wrong. If he rats people out, he will find himself and his family in the next highway project. Two weeks later, I met his friend Don Batiste. I got the name of his guy. We met and put him together with the unions he would be using. He got the bid where everybody shared in the job. Mr. Batiste was happy, his girlfriend was happy, and so was Mrs. Batiste.

Things went well, so I took my wife and met my friend Gregory and his wife at my favorite Russian restaurant in Brooklyn. We went there and saw our friend Nikolai had our little frozen vodka toast. Nikolai asked how come I don't do the parties anymore. He made his money from the girls I got from him. I said I was putting some other things together and I want to bring him in on it.

Nikolai asked if I could do him a favor; just ask, you know that. His son's girlfriend is getting a job in a strip club in Suffolk, and he needs someone to take her to the club and back to her apartment. "Why can't your son do it?" I asked.

"He is in jail in Russia for the next six months. He thought he would be out."

"If she has no problem, I can take care of it."

"Good," he says and calls her over. Jane comes to the table all 5'10" blonde blue-eyed Russian. I looked at my wife, and she was staring speechless. Jane said thank you and left.

Nikolai says, "Stupid young love." I asked Nikolai why the security people walking around looked so pissed off. He laughed as most are former KGB and now have no job, so they work here. No job security in Russia for them. They put on a great Vegas-like show with all the glitz music costumes.

There is no restaurant in New York that can match that kind of entertainment. We got ready to leave, I saw Nikolai, waved to him, and told him I would have the driver call him and make the arrangements. I reminded him I would be in touch business-wise in a week or two.

We had a good time, but as usual, I paid for it on the way home. I had to hear my wife carry on about why I have to bring shady activities into everything I do.

I hear this song and dance all the time, except when she is like the star. The perfect example to that was when the blockbuster movie *The Godfather* came out. Al Martino is doing a limited engagement at the San Su Sands club in Mineola. Shows are all sold out, no tickets available. My sister tells my wife, "That's too bad, it would have been nice." So now my wife says, "Ask your father. Maybe he knows someone." He makes a call and tells me to wait about an hour, call the club, and ask for Danny. I call and ask to speak to Danny, he is expecting my call. He says, "Come to the show on the second night. How many people?"

"Eight people, if possible."

"No problem. See you then." My mother, father, sister and her husband, her husband's brother and wife, and me and my wife.

We get there for the next night's final show, and it's obvious the table is up front and does not belong there—four feet from the microphone and the entertainer. Sal Richards, the comedian, comes out telling jokes, and because we are up front, he starts picking on my brother-in-law. Tells some Polish jokes then starts with Italian jokes. He suddenly stops, comes to the table, picks up a napkin, and wipes his forehead like he was sweating. I says, "I just realized why this table is here."

He says, "First of all, I don't own a horse, and I take back any jokes I made." People were laughing. He went on with his routine; he was great.

Al Martino came out and sang and at one point sang directly to the women at the table. He saw the album I brought and signed it. What clinched the possibility that this was a mob-related table is when he came over, took my father's hand, and kissed my mother on the cheek.

Those were the days!

When I got home, there was a message for me from a doctor friend of mine to call the office when I get a chance. I go to his office that Monday and tell the front desk the doctor asked me to come over to see him.

Ten minutes later, they show me to his office. He introduces me to the new doctor in his group. He says the new doctor has a problem that I can help him with. New guy tells me his family owns a restaurant, and they are having a problem with this couple that come to the restaurant. They made the typical fuss when people want to get a free meal. His sister apologized and said that there was no charge for the dinner and if they would please leave. They got up and left. He said my sister went out and got the plate number and make of the car. They came back the next day and said to my sister that they saw her write the plate number down. Then they said they would be back and throw acid in their face. She called the police, and they said they would check it out, but there was not much they could do. If they show again, he said call 911, and they will come right down. They did not come back, but they were making threatening calls. "Okay, give me the plate number, and I will take care of it," I said.

I got the address and went to visit them with an empty gas can and a lighter. I rang the bell and he came to the door. I was greeted with, "What the fuck do you want, asshole?"

I said that I came to talk to him about the restaurant people he was harassing.

He said he would have his biker friends ride all around the restaurant and nobody would go there anymore.

He did not pay attention to the gas can. I put the can down with the lighter. He said, "What the hell is that?" I gave him a piece of paper with my name and address on it, and the other two names are the guys who fixes his biker friends' bikes. They are also pagans. "Someone will be back with a full can of gas if you show up at the restaurant again. Understand? Do you have any other tough guys you are connected with?"

His response? "No, sir. We are very sorry. We will not go there anymore."

"Also, you will not call there anymore, correct?"

"Yes, sir. Correct."

"Thank you and have a good day."

I picked up my lighter and gas can and left. It freaks people out when you give them your name and address because it means you are a certified lunatic. I love doing this stuff.

Lucky finally got back to me with a few ideas. He wanted me to meet with his friend Tito in Sarasota. He has a charter fishing company in Florida and does regular runs to his hometown in Colombia. I said that it does not sound like anything can work out with this. "I can put him in contact with this local dealer I know. Your dealer is probably getting his cut-down coke from Tito anyway, so what else do you have? I have this Nigerian I met in prison who can get his hands on diamonds and emeralds. He needs someone to unload them for him. This we can do since my cousin is an expert in precious stones. I heard he was the one who came to my father's house to grade the jewels from the Lufthansa heist. The money was a mess from that, but the jewels the families divided it up I was told."

Lucky said, "Work on that, but in the meantime, we are going to send car parts to Cartegena. We sent two half containers down, made some money, but I did not think it was worth the hassle."

Lucky's wife had a store in Colombia where we sent clothes and small electronics. His wife wanted us to send her the two-ounce instant Maxwell House coffee. She said everybody loves it. I had an idea. I told Lucky we can send half a container of coffee for her to sell. We got the coffee to the shipping port in New Jersey and waited for the inspector to check and sign off on the bill of lading. He looked at us and said, "Do I look stupid? You want to send coffee to one of the biggest producers of coffee?"

I said, "Yes."

"So when I open these boxes, I will find instant coffee, correct?"

Lucky said, "Okay, open whatever you want and you can take a case for yourself." The inspector looked at us again and said, "You guys are either crazy or have the biggest set of balls." He signed off on the manifest and gave it back to Lucky. So off the coffee went to Colombia with 250,000 dollars stuffed in some of the jars.

I told Lucky, "I think I have the Nigerian thing all worked out."

He said, "Good. Now work on going to see that Tito brings in some nice money."

It's amazing how some people with money like to screw over the little guy. My friend Ernie is the perfect example. He went in business with a guy and Ernie's share was to clean out the old place, install the new equipment, make up menu's etc. He even used his credit card for small purchases. When the place opened, his friend paid him like a worker. Ernie said, "I thought we were partners."

"I paid you for your work. I own the place."

"I thought you drew up papers that I was a 50 percent owner."

"No," he said. "You were just a worker." Ernie came to me and asked what we could do. I said, "Nothing. He is too big with money. He has a lawyer, and you have no papers."

I felt bad for Ernie, and then I thought about it. I said, "Give me all the personal info you have on him—SSI number, home address, bank he deals with, his date of birth, etc." I passed it on to my friend in the CIA, and he put the information on the dark web. That is the CIA's go-to place when they want to screw people or organizations. I had him wipe some of his assets. I did not want to destroy him, just squeeze his balls to even the score for Ernie.

It actually worked in Ernie's favor. He was out quite a bit of money, so he asked Ernie to come back and help him. This time he put Ernie on paper as a 30 percent owner.

I needed a break from all this stress. I called my brother-in-law and told him we needed a vacation. Teddy says my wife and her sister decided they wanted to go to Lake George. Teddy has more friends and connections of anyone I have ever met. His cousins are the Gallos with that said. It explains, "If you need something, ask Teddy." The funny thing about Teddy is he has never broken a law in his life. His connections were so high up, he was, for two years, the driver for the governor of New York. The trip to Lake George was great; my wife and kids had a great time. I started to notice most places we went, Teddy knew the people. Lillian, my sister-in-law, said that's because they have been coming here for years.

One night, Teddy says we are going to a more fancy Italian eatery. I asked when we were sitting down. "Are you sure the food is good?"

"The best." We were through with dinner and checking out for dessert when some guy who looks like he should have the lead role in the godfather came up. Teddy gets up and hugs him. He says, "This is Santo. He owns the place." Santo calls the waitress over and tells her there would be no check for the table. Teddy makes a fuss telling him a round of drinks would be a nice gesture not the bill.

Santo tells Teddy, "With everything you do for me, this is nothing. Tell me, how is everything on Long Island?"

When we got back to our cabin, the lecture from my wife starts. "Can we ever go to a place where someone does not owe anyone?"

"Relax. This was Teddy's friend, not mine."

Back home, I told Lucky I was going down to Florida to see Tito.

He had a big-time operation going. He had charter fishing boats you can go for the day and others a five-day fishing excursion.

I told him Lucky was working on moving some of his product in the Queens-Jamica area. I asked him if he wanted to work with my Russian friend Nikolai. I told him Nikolai would take five kilos in the beginning, and if the product is good, he can move it. He would have taken more, but before the first scheduled transaction with Tito and Nikolai could take place, things fell apart. Nikolai got arrested for some fake loan company he set up for people needing to consolidate bills.

I did not tell Tito what happened because he would get paranoid that he was arrested. Then he would blame me if anything went wrong with his operation because the police got involved even though he had no communication with Nikolai.

Lucky still dabbled with Tito, but I started putting together the diamond deal with Lucky's friend from Guinea Equatorial. Bonner claimed to be able to get the stones here through diplomatic pouch. He has no place to unload them here or in London where he lived. I put everything and everyone together, and things were going smooth, or so I thought.

Lucky went back to Cartagena and worked at his wife's store. I stayed in touch with Tito and did some work for him.

Del and me had enough of this cowboy stuff, so we decided to open up a deli and be like normal businessmen. It worked good for a while, but nothing great. Once people knew where we were, and they started bringing in jewelry, electronics, and some antiques. I was turning into an unregistered pawnshop. We did better with this than the deli. One creative person brought in a large inventory from the local Burger King.

Del gets annoyed and says, "Why can't we go no more than five months before we turn illegal?"

I said, "Shut up and put Whoppers on the special menu."

That cracked Del up. He said, "Should we beat their price?"

"Of course. We are businessmen." We tried to sell the place but barely broke even.

The last job Del and I did was for my friend who owned a high-end men's store that carried all-Italian clothing. Sal told us to grab a suit or shirt tie; whatever we wanted as this job was a freebie. Del said he could not find anything that fit. I told him that's because not too many Italians are 6'5" and 300 lbs.

Lots of smoke damage and Sal got out on top. He split his store into three rentals and collected his rents.

Del said he was going to Arizona. His friend out there would set him up working for him.

I took Del out for dinner and drinks to wish him luck.

Del felt the need to give me some going-away advice from an old-time friend and partner.

Del knew stories I told him before we met and before our current episodes. He told me to stop trying to settle every petty insult or screwing I got. I said, "I don't."

He said, "Let me give you a recent perfect example. It seems you were in a restaurant in Brightwaters called the Duck Pond Inn. You said you were sitting at the bar and guys in their forties were talking, and that you heard part of the conversation. They were talking about stereotypes and ethnic names. They were drinking and getting loud, and one guy called you and said, *I bet your name is Tony*. I looked at the two of them and said, *No. Want to guess again?* You said the third guy who was no-joining in the conversation said, *Ignore them. Let me get you a drink*. I guess he saw the look in my eyes. That's when you called me and said you can't start your car, so come down with somebody to help. I said, *Be there in forty mins, I'm out East*. I was not. Just dragged me feet and waited 'til they would leave or you would cool off."

I agreed with him and said, "I am done with all this crap."

A month later, I get a call from Tito to come down to Sarasota. I get there, and he tells me he has a big problem. His niece's husband, Mikey, who runs his operation in the Bronx and Manhattan was skimming a big amount of coke. He checked with his people up in New York, and they told him Mikey was partying with his gay friends and handing out eight balls like Christmas. Worse was they were caught giving blow jobs. They told Tito that this did not look good for the operation. He wanted Mikey gone, but he did not want his niece to find out about this. I told him what we could do, and he agreed it was perfect. He called his boat captain and first mate to meet with us.

He told them that in the next trip to Colombia, his nephew and the Italian will be going with them. "The Italian will be in charge, and you do what he tells you. If anything happens to my Italian friend, you both better not come back. Understand?"

I told them that when we went to bring a diver's weight belt, Tito told Mikey to come down for the next trip to Colombia and that I was going with them. Two weeks later, we left for Colombia. Halfway to Colombia, the mate grabs and cuffs Mikey. Mikey starts screaming, "What the fuck is going on! Tito will have your heads for this!"

I tell the captain, "Cut the engine, and put the belt on Mikey." I hang him over the side, cut his throat, and toss him overboard. "Tell the captain start the engines and head for Colombia." I tell them the story will be that when we got to the border town, things went bad, Mikey was shot and killed, we barely got out, and were not able to get the shipment. "Make sure you both stick to this story, and Tito will give you extra cash for this trip." When we got back, I told him all went well and the captain and mate knew the story.

Tito told me that when I got back to New York, somebody will drop 10,000 for me. I reminded Tito, "Don't forget, 750 for two trips to Florida to resolve this"

Tito says, "Are you Italian or Jewish? You really want 750 more?"

"Yes. I have to pay my credit card when it comes in."

He laughed and said, "I'll have them drop 11,000 off to you."

I keep in touch with Tito from time to time, and he tells me they had a lovely service for Mikey. His niece said she knew that this would eventually happen.

Now I just want to spend time with my wife, kids, and grandkids. I want to concentrate on my regular work and put things behind me.

It never really ends. I still get calls for some work or a friend has a problem and wants to see if I can help. They come to me because they know *I know a guy who knows a guy*. Unlike my father, I did not pass any of these connections down to my sons. I told my sons and daughters to involve themselves with politicians and business people—these are the connections to have now. Mine and my father's time are gone like dinosaurs. They are gone, but you can read about them and wonder how life was back then. Stories my father would tell of respect and honor are a thing of the past. No one cares who you are or what you did. Now you are just an old man with his stories that nobody cares about or wants to hear about; even family.

Anyone hearing these stories may say how terrible these things were. In general, we kept these among criminals.

You read about Ponzi schemes where one person rips off people's life savings or online fraud where people's money they worked for is gone in an instant. In my opinion, that is a lot worse than the things the mob did.

They robbed Lufthansa, and the only victims were those involved. This was because of paranoia. Jewels made it to the Scalini house to be distributed, I was told. No innocent bystanders killed.

The Parkway gas taxes evasions scheme had no Russian/Italian injuries. Scalini house held on and moved a few missing millions I heard. Just business!

Oh and that London story went well. I landed in London, a cab takes me to the Kensington Hotel, and on the way the driver slows down and points out the MI6 building, which houses the British secret service. He says that this is where scenes from the James Bond movies were shot. Being a polite guy, I act very enthusiastic and ask if we can drive by it to get a better look. I said that I wish I had a camera. We drove along and he pointed out a few more things and suggested other places which I should see before I leave. I thank him and wanted to add that I can't stay long—that I'm on my way for a contract kill.

At the hotel, I check in, and there is a message for me. It said call when you arrive. I settled in and worked out my plan of action. Got something to eat and slept about an hour or two. Later in the evening, I went down to the front desk, checked out, and asked them to arrange a ride to Bonner's place. I then had them arrange another car to pick me up there in ninety minutes from the time the first car picks me up.

When I arrive at Bonner's place, he wasn't there just as we expected. Rufus, his brother, told me he was called away on an emergency family matter. We talked and he explained that we were even and everything that was agreed upon was delivered. I did not spend much time discussing this, my job was to send a message. I checked my watch and figured it was about time. I stood up, Rufus was sitting in front of me, I leaned on him with my left hand and with the right I shoved the knife in my hand up his diaphragm into his heart. I looked around, cleaned my knife, checked if I touched anything, and went outside. I have to admit I was impressed. Five minutes I waited outside, and the car was there to pick me up. I told him to take me to the airport and gave him extra on the fare just like a rich yank!

At the airport, I had them change my flight for the next flight to New York. Those were the days before 9/11, when things were easy to do. I waited through the night for my flight and home sweet home. Everything went smooth. I land at JFK, and who breaks my balls? The TSA security guy said he wants to know why I went to London. "Business or pleasure?"

I said, "Both."

"You flew seven thousand miles to come back in a day."

I said, "The person I was meeting is my friend and business partner. He became ill, so I had to leave." The only luggage I had was a garment bag. He opened it, looked and felt around, said okay, and let me pass. Funny thing going and coming back, nobody picked up on my knife at the bottom of the bag. Thank God this was all before 9/11.

Four weeks after I'm home, Jimmy tells me he got a package for the old man with the rest of the agreed-on diamonds. It pays to complain when you don't get your complete order. I have to say I work faster than a credit card dispute! I try to stay in the loop for connection. Most of my people are either dead or in jail. All the old-timers including my father are dead. The ones in jail won't be out until after I'm dead. I'm seventy-five, and most are looking at ten to twenty years away. I try to keep contacts in case my family and kids have a problem and need help.

Life breezes by like flashes in a dream. All the crazy days become a vague memory, and all you can do is reflect on the past and wonder how you survived! The glory days are over, now it's up to a new generation to make their memories. The memories they make will just be a watered-down version.

Recently, I was invited to my friend David's birthday party in Brentwood. It was quite a gathering of friends and family. The variety of South American cuisine made it look like a fiesta instead of a simple birthday party. David introduced me to his family and friends that I had not met. I was treated like family. One particular group of his friends were sitting off to the side. You can tell they were a serious bunch and evidently well respected.

The group kept to themselves, drank, and talked among themselves. Occasionally they looked over toward where I sat. The older one of the five got up and started walking over to me. I am thinking I am going to be asked to leave. Instead, he shakes my hand and says, "Thank you for coming. Welcome to our family." One at a time, the other four came over, introduced themselves, and said welcome.

Later when I saw David, I told him that I thought I was going to be asked to leave.

David said, "I told him how we met and things we worked on. Your age and your background is the reason for that gesture of respect." I guess nationality and cultural background respect still had its place. It felt nice to respected. Like my father said, "Give respect and get respected."

Rufus, as per my attorney and my partners, the power of attorney cannot be signed. This leaves no control over money and distributions. Send 10 percent of the amount to me in US dollars or the equivalent in precious stone. I will send the power of attorney, and the money distribution will be totally left in your hands. When this matter is finally settled, I will come down and settle all issues with Mr. Uzo Okeke, as to ensure your safety. We must come to a money agreement, so e-mail me with any suggestions you may have.

Thanks,
Al

Please call me so that I can give you his telephone and fax numbers.

I am writing to hear from you ASAP.

Remain blessed.

Prince Rufus Okwarauba

208 Road B close
House 11
Festac Town-Lagos
Nigeria
234-1-884711

Dear Al,

Why have you refused to call me for a long time now? I have been trying to contact you for the past month without success. Did you change your telephone and fax numbers without letting me know? My not being able to reach you through your numbers has necessitated me to write you.

Please get in touch with me immediately once you receive this letter. Give me your recent telephone and fax number including your email address, if any, for easier communication. My email address is RHYKWANIGLIO@excite.com.

I have concluded arrangement to send you stones from two sources. They are prepared to send stones by my guarantee which they are expecting their money after you must have finished sales. One of the sources is also prepared to come down to America for the sales. I have also carried your ___ the American.

Still kept my travel souvenir.

```
HOTEL LONDON HEATHROW              OUT-24NOV
SRS-WORLDHOTELS                    2 NIGHTS
THE KENSINGTON                     1 ROOM      AMERICAN EXPRESS
KESINGTON HOUSE RICHMOND WAY       RATE-112.00GBP PER NIGHT
LONDON W14 0AX                     CANCEL BY 02P DAY OF ARRIVAL
UNITED KINGDOM
FONE 44-171-674-1000226
FAX  44-171-674-1050
GUARANTEED LATE ARRIVAL
CONFIRMATION 7209834
REQ NONSMOKING


SGAMBATI/ALFONSO    AMERICAN EXPRESS    623-492-5000    SGTBHR  3
```

EXECUTIVE CORPORATE TRAVEL SERVICE

Advantages that travel wherever, whenever you do.
Exclusively for Executive Corporate Cardmembers.

Executive Referral and Information Services for travelers:
Anything an executive might require – from an office for the day in Dallas to a translator for a meeting in Japan.

A worldwide network of travel locations:*
Over 1,700 American Express travel locations are waiting to serve you, across the U.S. and in more than 120 countries around the world.

One 24-hour toll-free number for anything, everything:
One call will put a specially trained Executive Assistant to work for you… for new reservations, to help you with any change of plans, or for any business assistance you may require while you're away from work staff.

```
BRITISH AIRWAYS

SGAMBATI
311833
LONDON

LGW BA 2172           672
BA 674663
     0128
```

```
21 NOV 99   -  SUNDAY
            INFORMATION
            CITIZENS OF THE UNITED STATES MUST CARRY A VALID PASSPORT
            BRITISH AIRWAYS        FLT:2172    BUSINESS
            LV NEW YORK JFK                    615P          FQP: 777
            DEPART: TERMINAL 7                               07HR 05MIN

22 NOV 99   -  MONDAY
            AR LONDON    GATWICK              620A          NON-STOP
            ARRIVE: NORTH TERMINAL                          REF: TULNKY
            SGAMBATI/ALFONS    SEAT-16B


SGAMBATI/ALFONSO      AMERICAN EXPRESS        623-492-5000
```

EXECUTIVE
CORPORATE
TRAVEL
SERVICE

Advantages that travel wherever, whenever you do.
Exclusively for Executive Corporate Cardmembers.

*Executive Referral and Information Services
for travelers:*
Anything an executive might require – from an office for
the day in Dallas to a translator for a meeting in Japan.

*A worldwide network of
travel locations*:*
Over 1,700 American Express travel locations are
waiting to serve you, across the U.S. and in more than
120 countries around the world.

*One 24-hour toll-free number-
for anything, everything:*
One call will put a specially trained Executive Assistant
to work for you… for new reservations, to help you with
any change of plans, or for any business assistance you
may require while you're away from your staff.

9 7 9 8 8 8 7 6 3 1 8 7 5